✳ Smithsonian

VOLCANO
WHERE FIRE AND WATER MEET

BY MARY M. CERULLO

CAPSTONE EDITIONS
a capstone imprint

To Justine Glynn and Gary Lewis,
who made my Hawaii adventure possible —MMC

Published by Capstone Editions, an imprint of Capstone.
1710 Roe Crest Drive
North Mankato, Minnesota 56003
capstonepub.com

Library of Congress Cataloging-in-Publication Data is available on the Library of Congress website.
ISBN: 9781684462063 (hardcover)
ISBN: 9781684469550 (paperback)
ISBN: 9781684462070 (ebook PDF)

Summary: Lava shoots into the air, then bubbles down mountains, flattening, burning, and boiling everything in its path. The destructive forces of volcanoes are terrifying and well-known. But what about their other forces? Award-winning children's science author Mary M. Cerullo brings her excellent research and signature storytelling style to the dynamic subject of volcanoes. Stitching science, history, and mythology together, Cerullo explores these explosive wonders of nature and reveals the secrets they've been keeping since the beginning of the world.

Image Credits: Alamy: John De Mello, 33 (inset); Capstone: 6 (bottom left) and throughout, 21 (bottom inset); Dreamstime: Britta Harris, 32 (bottom), Marlon Trottmann, 24 (bottom); NASA: 43 (right inset); National Park Service: Hawaii Volcanoes National Park, 7 (top), 17 (middle left); Newscom: BSIP, 11 (bottom), Danita Delimont Photography/David R. Frazier, 43 (left inset), Dave Fleetham, 32 (middle), Design Pics/Dave Fleetham, 38 (bottom right); National Oceanic and Atmospheric Administration: NOAA Okeanos Explorer Program/Galapagos Rift Expedition 2011, 41 (middle inset), NOAA Okeanos Explorer Program/Our Deepwater Backyard, 28 (bottom), NOAA Vent Program/Image Courtesy of Submarine Ring of Fire 2006 Exploration, 40, 41 (back and top right inset); Shutterstock: Adam Nettleton, 37 (top), bearacreative, 37 (inset), Benny Marty, 2-3, 22 (bottom), Bos11, 16, Bule Sky Studio, 18 (bottom left), Darren J. Bradley, 38 (top left), Designua, 14 (bottom), Dmitry Pichugin, 19 (bottom right), Enguerrand Cales (lava design element), 4 (top) and throughout, EnviroSense, 19 (top left), eshoot, 39 (middle right), Evan Austen, endsheets, Everett Collection, 15 (top), Fabio Lamanna, 36 (middle), FCG, 13 (bottom), feygraphy, 18 (top left), foto-select, 17 (bottom), Fredy Thuerig, cover (top), 5, George Burba, 4, Hiroyuki Saita, 39 (middle left), Javrob, 18 (bottom right), jo Crebbin, 33 (back), Joe Belanger, 44-45, Johan Swanepoel, 10 (bottom left), 12 (front), Juergen Wallstabe, 17 (top), Karoline Cullen, 39 (top left), Katy Foster, 36 (bottom), Lokuttara, 35 (bottom), Love Lego, 35 (top), Luc Kohnen, 18 (top right), mapichai, 20 (inset), Martin Voeller, 38 (top right), Meister Photos, 30, Miloje (grunge background), 15 (bottom) and throughout, MNStudio, 21 (top inset), 28 (top), Nataliia K (water background), 24 (top) and throughout, nikkytok, 1, 46-47, 48, Nina B, 28 (middle), Noel Powell, back cover (top), Pavel Gabzdyl, 10 (top), Peter Bardocz, 22-23 (map), Peter Hermes Furian, 13 (top), 25 (right), Petr Klabal, cover and back cover (bottom), Photovolcanica, 17 (middle right), PsychoBeard, cover and back cover texture, Rajneesh Kumar Thakur, 36 (illustrations), RelentlessImages, 7 (middle), Roberto Politi, 19 (top right), Robin Runck, 42-43, RobJ808, 38 (bottom left), rudvi (pattern), 8-9 (bottom), 21 (bottom), 22-23 (top and bottom), 40-41 (bottom), S_E, 18-19 (map), Shane Myers Photography, 39 (bottom right), Smelov, 8-9 (top), sripfoto, 10 (back), 12 (back), srisondem, 11 (back), Steve Heap, 39 (bottom left), Tara Schulz, 7 (bottom), Tatsiana Kuryanovich, 15 (bottom right), Timothy Ewing, 39 (top right), tunasalmon, 14 (top), VectorMine, 17 (volcano type insets), Volina, 20-21 (back), Wead, 19 (middle right), Wouter van de Kamp, 25 (left), Zamir Popat, 19 (middle left); USGS: 6-7, 26-27, 29, 31 (bottom), Hawaiian Volcano Observatory, 26 (bottom), 31 (top), 34

Editor: Kristen Mohn; Designer: Sarah Bennett; Media Researcher: Svetlana Zhurkin, Production Specialist: Katy LaVigne

Our very special thanks to Benjamin J. Andrews, Director, Global Volcanism Program, Department of Mineral Sciences, National Museum of Natural History, Smithsonian Institution. Capstone would also like to thank Kealy Gordon, Product Development Manager, and the following at Smithsonian Enterprises: Jill Corcoran, Director, Licensed Publishing; Brigid Ferraro, Vice President, Education and Consumer Products; and Carol LeBlanc, President, Smithsonian Enterprises.

All internet sites appearing in back matter were available and accurate when this book was sent to press.

Printed and bound in China. PO5378

CONTENTS

INTRODUCTION

It is eerily quiet. No birds are singing. The streets are deserted. The countryside looks like a scene from a fantasy movie where fire-breathing dragons burned or trampled everything in sight.

Kilauea (KILL-ah-WAY-ah), on the island of Hawaii, has been called the most active volcano in the world. It erupted continuously, but gently, for 35 years. Curious tourists would crowd the edge of the volcano to stare into the crater. Far below, fiery, molten rock spurted between black streaks of cooling lava.

Lava from Kilauea covered homes in the town of Pahoa.

Kilauea erupted throughout the summer of 2018.

Even as visitors were thrilled by the display, scientists in charge of monitoring the volcano were becoming alarmed. For more than six months, their sensors had been detecting pressure building up deep inside the volcano's magma chamber.

On May 3, 2018, that magma forced its way up through multiple cracks along the slopes of the volcano. Rivers of lava streamed down to the sea, burying homes, roads, and tropical forests in their path.

Thankfully, no humans died in the 2018 eruption. The lava moved slowly enough for people to move out of its path. But their homes could not move. The lava buried or burned about 700 structures.

Five months after the eruption ended, the landscape looked alien and mysterious. The smell of rotten eggs still lingered. A volcanic fog of steam and poisonous sulfuric acid, called vog, hovered just above the ground. Hot steam vents dotted the jagged, uneven lava fields. Bits of hardened lava foam called volcanic ash covered the ground. Earthquakes that occurred hundreds of times a day during the massive eruption had mostly stopped, but small tremors continued.

The Leilani Estates neighborhood was in the path of the lava flow of the 2018 eruption.

FACT
Molten rock is called magma while it is inside the earth. Once it reaches the surface and flows out of the volcano, it is called lava.

'Ae fern growing in the lava field

Yet signs of life were evident within months. Bright green ferns poked through the cooled lava—new life growing from the ash. A bulldozer had leveled a home so its owners could rebuild. Not far away, construction crews were repaving roads where earthquakes had torn gaping holes in the earth.

Out in the ocean, where tide pools and coral reefs lie buried under fresh lava, minerals from the ash and lava provide nutrients for new life. Just as fertilizers encourage the growth of vegetables in a garden, these nutrients jump-start the growth of tiny marine plants. The plants provide food for the rest of the ocean food web.

It is a reminder that destruction and creation go hand-in-hand wherever volcanoes are found.

Purple sea urchins in the tide pool

AN ANCIENT CONNECTION

Hawaiian tradition dating back more than a thousand years states that all life began in the ocean. According to folklore, all living things—including humans—are tied to marine life.

In fact, that is more than folklore. That is science. Volcanoes, like the ones that the Hawaiian people have lived alongside for generations, lit the spark of life on planet Earth. Without volcanoes, there would be no life here—not one person, animal, plant, or even the tiniest microscopic bacteria.

How can that be?

To find out why, we need to go back. Way back to the early stages of Earth's existence.

Scientists estimate that Earth is 4.5 billion years old. Early on, it was not a welcome place for humans or any other living thing. The still-forming planet was pelted by space rubble and battered by solar winds. Those things prevented any breathable atmosphere from sticking around. Many millions of years passed before a stable atmosphere evolved.

How did life on Earth happen?

VOLCANIC ERUPTIONS!

VOLCANOES ONCE COVERED EARTH, FLOODING
THE ENTIRE GLOBE WITH A SEA OF MOLTEN MAGMA.

Their eruptions released water vapor and other gases from inside the earth. Asteroids and icy comets hitting the planet added more gases to the mix. Together, the gases created an atmosphere mostly made up of:

• water vapor (water that is in the form of a gas)

• carbon dioxide (what we exhale when we breathe)

• methane gas (still the most abundant gas in the atmosphere today, and not just because cows burp tons of it)

As Earth's atmosphere cooled, the water vapor condensed into thick clouds of water droplets. Then rain fell and filled the basins that are now our oceans. Our first oceans were fresh water. Constant rains eventually washed minerals off the land. The minerals dissolved into the oceans, making them salty.

It was in the oceans that life evolved. Ancient sea creatures— simple, one-celled plants—used the energy of the sun to break apart carbon dioxide into carbon and oxygen in seawater. This process eventually created an atmosphere in which animals, including humans, could breathe.

Single-celled organisms in the oceans called stromatolites were among the first living things on Earth.

WHAT'S GOING ON UNDERGROUND?

Volcanoes spew fiery lava, pulverized rocks, and black clouds of ash and poisonous gas. They have their beginnings deep inside the earth.

Earth has three layers. Think of them like the parts of an egg:

- the **crust** (the eggshell), the outermost layer, which is broken into many jagged plates

- the **mantle** (the egg white), which is filled with semifluid material that can ooze like slime

- the **core** (the yolk), which is a very dense mass of hot metals such as iron and nickel

crust

mantle

core

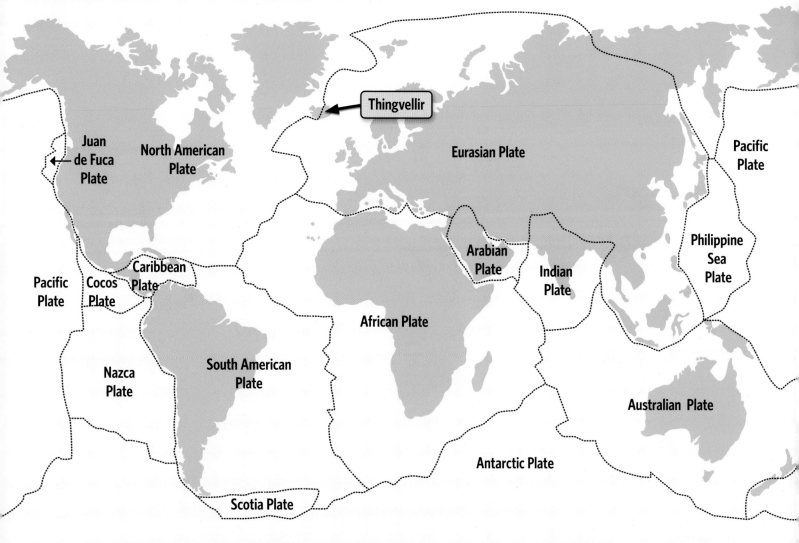

The cracked surface is divided into tectonic plates, which slowly drift around the globe. You might think of these plates as rafts carried by currents of superheated magma. They grind against each other and occasionally snap and jerk apart, creating powerful earthquakes.

The plates normally move only a few centimeters a year—about as fast as your fingernails grow. Yet they can push up mountain chains or create deep valleys and ocean trenches thousands of miles long.

Thingvellir National Park in Iceland, at the tectonic divide between the North American and the Eurasian plates

THE RING OF FIRE

RING OF FIRE

PACIFIC OCEAN

The region that surrounds the edge of the Pacific Ocean is called the "Ring of Fire." It's named for the many earthquakes and volcanic eruptions that happen there. The Pacific Plate is a massive slab of Earth's crust that lies beneath the Pacific Ocean. It bumps up against other tectonic plates to the west, north, and east. In several places, the Pacific Plate dives into the mantle beneath the other plates, pulling pieces of the continents with it.

In other places, plate grinds against plate, like football players trying to muscle past each other. Along the west coast of North America is the North American Plate's boundary. The plate moves south, grating against the Pacific Plate, which moves in the opposite direction. They may lock up until a sudden movement, like an earthquake along the San Andreas Fault, gets them unstuck.

Types of Plate Boundaries

Convergent Plate Boundary
where two plates collide and one
eventually slides beneath the other

Transform Plate Boundary
where two plates are moving
past each other

Divergent Plate Boundary
where two plates are moving
away from each other

Roads split apart during the San Francisco earthquake of 1906.

The results can be disastrous. In California, the San Francisco earthquake of 1906 destroyed nearly 500 city blocks. It left half of the city's residents homeless and 3,000 dead. Whenever tectonic plates dive, grind, or split, something big happens.

Famous Volcanoes Around the Ring of Fire

Around the Ring of Fire are several volcanoes famous for their eruptions: Mount Fuji in Japan, Mount Pinatubo in the Philippines, Krakatau in Indonesia, Mount St. Helens in the United States, and Popocatépetl in Mexico. Some of the 452 volcanoes along the Ring of Fire have not erupted for a very long time. U.S. geoscientists keep a close watch on ones in Alaska, Washington state, Oregon, and California—many of which would threaten nearby cities if they erupted.

Popocatépetl

CLASSIFYING VOLCANOES

(Hint: Look at the Shape)

Shield volcanoes, like those in Hawaii, have gentle slopes shaped like the rounded shields of ancient warriors. They are created as more and more layers of lava build up over time. Eruptions of Hawaii's shield volcanoes are normally less destructive than other kinds of volcanoes.

Cinder cones are the simplest type of volcano. Gas-filled lava is shot out of a vent and then falls as blobs of lava—or cinders—which build up a steep-sided cone. Cinder cones are usually only up to about 1,000 feet (305 meters) tall.

Lava domes are rounded cones often found inside craters or on the sides of larger composite volcanoes because their lava is too thick to flow far.

Stratovolcanoes, also called composite volcanoes, are steep-sided cones that can release massive ash clouds, gas, and debris during explosive eruptions. They can also erupt as lava flows or domes. These volcanoes often generate deadly mud flows called lahars.

FACT

How do scientists determine if a volcano is active, dormant, or extinct?

Active: having erupted, or at least disturbed the peace, within the past 10,000 years

Dormant: has not been active within the past 10,000 years but *could* be

Extinct: has not been active in the past 10,000 years and lacks the ability to become so

Arenal in Costa Rica is a dormant volcano.

Mauna Kea in Hawaii

shield volcano

Puu Puai in Hawaii

cinder cone

Rerombola in Indonesia

lava dome

Arenal in Costa Rica

stratovolcano

READY TO RUMBLE

More than 1,400 volcanoes on our planet are classified as active. Here are some of the ones that volcano scientists, called volcanologists, and the volcanoes' neighbors are keeping an eye on.

Krakatau (also called Krakatoa) is a volcano in Indonesia. In 1883, it exploded in one of the greatest eruptions in recorded history. Gases and debris shot as far as 50 miles (80 kilometers) into the atmosphere. Since 1927, another stratovolcano has been growing and erupting on a new island— Anak Krakatau, meaning "Child of Krakatau."

The Hawaiian Islands are made up of active, dormant, and extinct shield volcanoes. **Mauna Loa, Hualālai,** and **Kilauea** are considered active.

Mount Fuji, in Japan, last erupted in 1707, but recent earthquake activity suggests that magma is on the move below the surface. This stratovolcano could erupt again, but probably not tomorrow. Mount Fuji sits at the intersection of three tectonic plates, a dangerous place to be!

Popocatépetl (Aztec for "smoking mountain") is in Mexico. It is a stratovolcano that erupts quite often, and it's not far from major cities, including Mexico City. A destructive eruption would put millions of people at risk.

Mount Erebus has been active for about 1.3 million years! Not many people pay attention to its eruptions, except for the explorers and scientists who visit the polar region of Antarctica. This volcano is a shield volcano on its bottom half and a stratovolcano on the top half.

Mount Stromboli, located on a small island south of Italy, has been erupting almost continuously for 2,000 years. At night, its explosive eruptions can be seen far away, earning this stratovolcano the nickname "Lighthouse of the Mediterranean."

Piton de la Fournaise (French for "Peak of the Furnace") is a shield volcano in the Indian Ocean on Réunion Island, a part of France. It has erupted more than 150 times in the past 500 years. Locals call it simply *Le Volcan*.

Mount Etna is a stratovolcano on the east coast of Sicily, an island of Italy. Etna is in an almost constant state of eruption. Ash from its eruptions has drifted as far north as Rome, 500 miles (800 km) away.

Mount Ruapehu, in New Zealand, is part of the Ring of Fire. This stratovolcano sits where the denser Pacific Plate slides beneath the Australian Plate.

HAWAIIAN HOT SPOT

Nowhere is the connection between fire and water more evident than in Hawaii. The Hawaiian volcanoes are not part of the Ring of Fire that encircles the Pacific Ocean. They are closer to the middle of the Pacific Ocean and sit atop a crack in the mantle called a hot spot. There, plumes of magma rise through the ocean floor to become volcanoes. A plume starts very deep within the earth, where the core and mantle meet. As the superheated plume rises through the mantle, it melts. This forms the magma that eventually erupts as a volcano.

How Hot Spots Form New Islands

A volcano erupts on the seabed—molten rock breaks through Earth's crust.

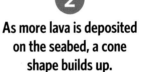
As more lava is deposited on the seabed, a cone shape builds up.

The lava breaks the water's surface, forming a new island.

Mauna Kea and Mauna Loa are located on the Big Island of Hawaii.

Mauna Loa rises above the clouds.

Mauna Loa   Mt. Rainier

Pacific Ocean

If Mt. Rainier in Washington grew from the ocean floor like Mauna Loa, Mauna Loa would dwarf Rainier.

In fact, the Hawaiian Islands *are* volcanic mountains. They began erupting on the ocean floor. Over time, through many eruptions, they continued to grow until their peaks broke the water's surface. Measured from the sea floor to their peaks, two of them—Mauna Kea and Mauna Loa—are the tallest mountains in the world!

The Pacific Plate slides slowly northwest at a rate of about 1.5 inches (4 centimeters) a year. It pulls the Hawaiian Islands with it. Scientists estimate it took about a million years each for the five main islands of Hawaii to move across the hot spot and rise up out of the ocean.

Now another volcano is growing above the hot spot. Loihi is more than 2 miles (3.2 km) tall and growing by inches every year. For now, it is still underwater. Loihi should reach the surface in 10,000 to 100,000 years to become Hawaii's newest island.

The Hawaiian Islands will erode away and become part of the sea again, many millions of years from now. The western Hawaiian Islands of Kauai and Oahu are already showing the signs of old age—extinct or dormant volcanoes and worn-down mountains.

The Big Island, also called the island of Hawaii, is the youngest and most volcanically active member of the island chain. It is also the easternmost island in Hawaii . . . at least until Loihi rises above the water.

Niihau

Kauai

Kaula

PACIFIC

OCEAN

FACT

There are other hot spots around the world. Yellowstone in Wyoming is one of them. Geysers and hot springs are clues that a system of gigantic magma chambers lies not far below the surface. Geologists call it a supervolcano. It could devastate the landscape around it and affect the weather worldwide if it erupts. Past eruptions of Yellowstone's massive supervolcano pumped volcanic gases high into the atmosphere, cooling the entire planet for years.

Castle Geyser erupting in Yellowstone National Park

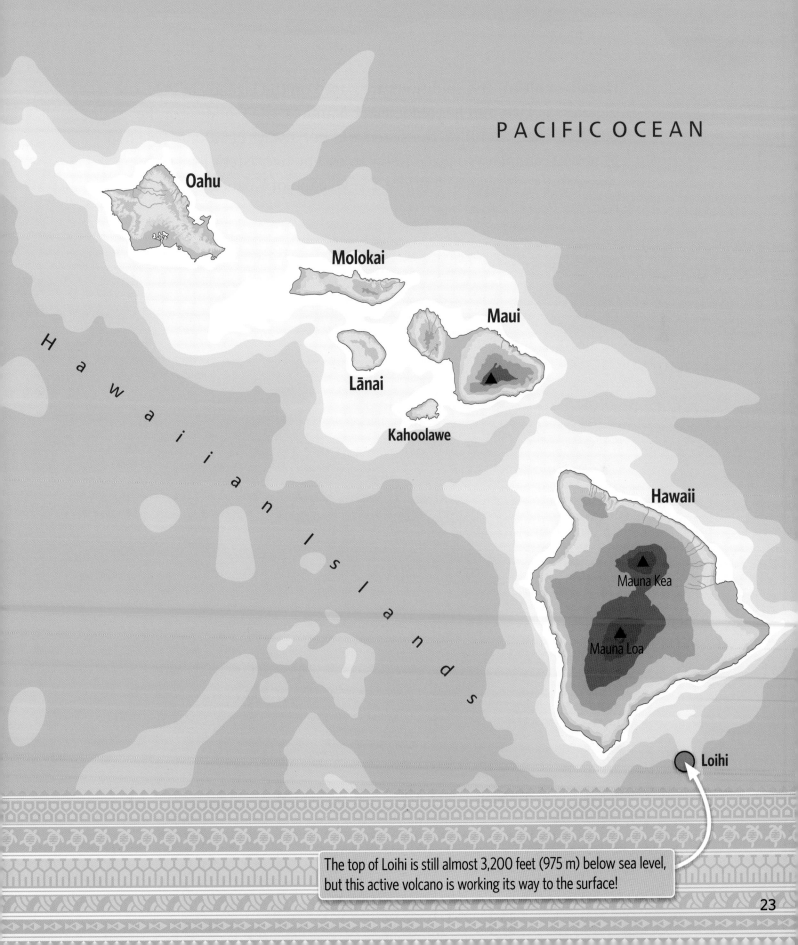

PACIFIC OCEAN

Oahu

Molokai

Maui

Lānai

Kahoolawe

Hawaii

Mauna Kea

Mauna Loa

Loihi

Hawaiian Islands

The top of Loihi is still almost 3,200 feet (975 m) below sea level, but this active volcano is working its way to the surface!

PELE WAKES

Hawaii's culture and traditions are based on the legends of Pele, the Goddess of Fire, and her older sister Nāmaka, the Goddess of the Sea. Like many families, the sisters did not always get along. Pele had to move from place to place to try to escape her sister's jealous rage. According to Hawaiian folklore, the volcano of Kilauea eventually became Pele's home.

Mural of the Goddess Pele

From time to time, Pele tosses out lava to roll over the land and churn the sea. Hawaiians take it in stride. They leave fruit, flowers, and other tributes on stone altars to appease Pele and show their acceptance of a force they cannot control.

Pele's home of Kilauea sits on the side of a much bigger volcano, Mauna Loa. It is one of five volcanoes on the island of Hawaii. Although Mauna Loa and Kilauea have erupted explosively many times in their history, most recent eruptions have been quiet. These gradually build up layer after layer of lava across the land. Tourists could stand close to the edge of the crater of Kilauea to watch the mild eruptions.

Then,
in 2018,
Pele stirred up
TROUBLE.

Grading the Big Island's Volcanoes

Three of the five volcanoes on the Big Island are considered active.

• Kilauea (last erupted in 2020)
• Mauna Loa (last erupted in 1984)
• Hualālai (last erupted in 1801)

Kohala last erupted 120,000 years ago, so geologists feel confident calling it extinct. Volcanologists estimate that Mauna Kea last erupted around 2460 BCE, nearly 5,000 years ago. Should it be considered dormant? Scientists are reluctant to say so. After all, 5,000 years is just a blink of an eye in geologic time.

▲ Kohala

▲ Mauna Kea

Hilo ○

▲ Hualālai

Island of Hawaii

Mauna Loa ▲

▲
Kilauea
Hawaii Volcanoes
National Park

On May 3, 2018, the ground around Kilauea began to shake—a lot! Registering magnitude 6.9 on the Richter scale, it was the largest earthquake to take place in Hawaii in 43 years. It even generated a minor tsunami, a destructive ocean wave caused by an underwater earthquake or volcanic eruption.

Following the large earthquake, new pathways for magma opened up within the volcano. Lava escaped through new fissures in the volcano. Fiery fountains shot hundreds of feet into the air. More cracks continued to spread down the slope.

By the end of the eruption, 24 fissures had created new routes for lava to rampage across the landscape. This eruption was not like the mild-mannered eruptions that Hawaiians were used to. Two thousand islanders were forced to flee. Poisonous fumes made it too dangerous to stay anywhere close to the fissures.

Along with scalding steam, the vog contained sulfur dioxide, carbon dioxide, and particles of glass. The volcano even created its own weather. Heavy rain was a daily occurrence. As much as 10 inches (25 cm) of rain fell in one day.

Plumes of steam and sulfur dioxide rising from the fissures and into the clouds

At times, lava from this fissure in the lower east rift zone reached heights of about 160 feet (50 m).

By the time the eruption stopped three months later on August 4, the volcano had spewed out enough lava to cover nearly 14 square miles (36 sq km). It filled in Kapoho Bay, creating 1.4 square miles (3.6 sq km) of new land.

The floor of the caldera—a basin or crater inside the volcano—had dropped by 1,640 feet (500 m). If you peered into it today, you might just see steam rising through blackened lava. It is hard to imagine that this volcano erupted explosively for more than 90 days, blasting ash clouds high into the sky, to altitudes where airplanes fly.

pahoehoe lava

Types of Hawaiian Lava

It's easy to trace the paths of different eruptions. The newest lava is shiny black. It is much darker than older lava flows, which have weathered into various shades of chocolate. The fresh lava is coated with a thin layer of glass, giving its surface a silvery sheen.

Geologists in Hawaii identify Hawaiian lava as basalt, a fine-grained igneous rock. Basalt lavas come in three main forms:

a'a lava

Pahoehoe (paw-HOY-hoy) rises from the ground as a syrupy river of lava before hardening into smooth, ropey rock. Pahoehoe means "soft" in Hawaiian.

A'ā (ah-AH) is a gritty, sharp-edged type of lava that forms when the erupting lava becomes so sticky, or viscous, that it breaks into blocks as it flows.

pillow lava

Pillow lava forms only underwater. Cold seawater quenches the outside of the hot lava, making a shape like a throw pillow. The addition of more lava inside the pillow ultimately makes a crack that allows a new pillow to bud or form from the first pillow.

Aerial view of volcanic activity at Kilauea's caldera after the 2018 eruption

WHEN FIRE AND WATER MEET

Hot lava and water often react explosively when they meet. Clouds of ash, water vapor, sulfur dioxide, carbon dioxide, and lava chunks are launched high into the air. This lava haze, called laze, may contain hydrochloric acid and tiny slivers of volcanic glass—not safe for creatures on land or sea.

The temperature of lava is many times the boiling point of water. The heat can harm the animals and plants that can't move out of its path, such as many of those living in tide pools and coral reefs.

Lava from Fissure 8 entering Kapoho Bay

One of the greatest losses to nature from Kilauea's eruption was the destruction of a rare tide pool in Kapoho Bay. Natural lava walls surrounding a shallow basin had created a nursery area for small fish, sheltering them from bigger predators. It was a popular spot for snorkeling.

Waiʻōpae Tide Pool was so unique that it was protected as a Marine Life Conservation District by the state of Hawaii. In June 2018, a river of lava sprang from Fissure 8. It engulfed entire neighborhoods as it rolled down to the sea and over the Waiʻōpae Tide Pool 8 miles (12.9 km) away.

Scientists had been studying this ecosystem for 12 years. They had cataloged 82 species of fish, 10 different kinds of coral, and 17 species of invertebrates—animals without backbones like sea stars, spiny lobsters, and sea cucumbers. The tide pool was destroyed within 36 hours.

before eruption

after eruption

Kapoho, a town on the eastern tip of the Big Island, is now deserted after lava from Kilauea flooded much of the area.

Before Kilauea's 2018 eruption, marine biologist Misaki Takabayashi had been monitoring the health of the corals in the Wai'ōpae Tide Pool. Like most people who have lived in Hawaii, she accepts that volcanoes destroy—and create:

> "THE LAND IS BRAND-NEW, AND THERE WILL BE
> ANOTHER CORAL REEF SOON ENOUGH."

Another marine scientist, Steve Colbert, is studying how the lava has affected conditions in nearby coastal waters. He and colleagues monitor changes in water clarity, temperature, and acidity via a robot sub. Although recovery of the area could take centuries, he shared a positive outlook:

> "THERE'S GOING TO BE RENEWAL THAT COMES IN,
> AND IT'S GOING TO BE FANTASTIC TO SEE WHAT THAT IS AND HOW
> THIS ECOSYSTEM TRANSFORMS ITSELF INTO SOMETHING NEW."

Researchers studying the health of Hawaii's coral reefs

Seagoing Robot Rides the Waves

One of the coolest tools that researchers used was a robot called a wave glider. It floated on the ocean's surface like a paddle board, zigzagging along the shoreline where the lava was flowing into the water. Instruments measured air and water conditions as they were changing, allowing researchers to safely collect

RECOVERY

SO HOW DOES NATURE RECOVER? AND HOW LONG DOES IT TAKE?

Lava flow formed a new land area in the Pacific Ocean 875 acres (354 hectares) in size.

New Land

Some changes happen very quickly. Lava from the 2018 eruption of Kilauea transformed ocean into new land nearly the size of 700 football fields. New sand beaches are forming along the shoreline that was once Waiʻōpae Tide Pool. Lava from many previous eruptions has eroded into black sand along the entire coast of Hawaii.

Over time, rainwater and plants break down lava into soil. Minerals in the lava contain important nutrients, such as iron and phosphorus. These make volcanic soil ripe for growing lush forests, productive farms, vineyards, and orchards on the slopes of many active volcanoes. Some volcanic deposits elsewhere in the world contain minerals of even greater value, such as gold, copper, and diamonds.

Food for the Ocean

Just as nutrients from the lava help crops grow on land, the minerals also provide a growth spurt for plant life in the ocean. An unexpected benefit of the 2018 eruption of Kilauea was discovered in satellite images of the areas where lava and volcanic ash flowed into the sea. Scientists concluded that minerals in the lava were fertilizing massive blooms of algae large enough to be seen from space. These tiny floating plants feed other sea creatures throughout the ocean food web.

microscopic marine algae

A plantation of coffee trees, which thrive in volcanic soil, on the Big Island

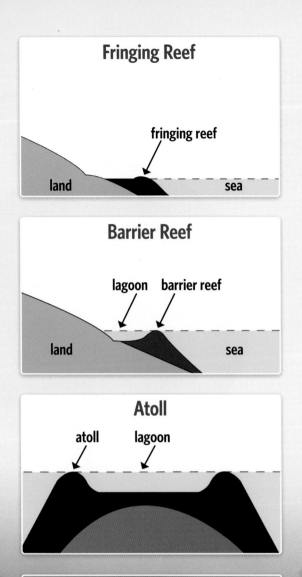

Fringing Reef

fringing reef

land   sea

Barrier Reef

lagoon barrier reef

land   sea

Atoll

atoll lagoon

an atoll

An Anchor for Corals

Other signs of recovery take a bit more time—or a *lot* more time.

Volcanic slopes make ideal habitats for growing corals. Corals need warm, relatively shallow water to get enough sunlight and wave action to thrive. The coral-volcano partnership begins when corals attach to the seaward edge of a volcano. They form a fringing reef. As the coral reef grows upward—and as the volcano sinks—a barrier reef forms. Barrier reefs are farther offshore, separated from land by a shallow lagoon. Eventually, the top of the volcano sinks below sea level. This process leaves behind an atoll, which is an irregularly shaped ring of coral with a lagoon in the middle.

The whole process, from fringing reef to atoll, may take as long as 30 million years. Hawaiian volcanoes are still youngsters in geological time. Its reefs are at the early stage of coral reef formation. They are still either fringing reefs or small, isolated patches of coral.

Coral reef in Hanauma Bay, on the south shore of Oahu, Hawaii

coral polyps

Coral Partners

Coral reefs are the creation of two main actors:
• small, vase-shaped animals called coral polyps
• tiny plant companions called zooxanthellae

Zooxanthellae are phytoplankton—tiny plants that live inside a thin layer of tissue that connects a colony of coral polyps. These creatures are related to jellyfish and sea anemones. Like their relatives, coral polyps capture their prey with stinging tentacles. Because the coral cannot move, they depend on wave action and currents to deliver their food.

FACT
The Hawaiian expression *malama i ke kai* means to care for or protect the ocean.

37

MEET HAWAII'S REEF DWELLERS

Hawaii's long history of volcanic eruptions has provided homes for 5,500 known kinds of marine plants and animals. They live in coral reefs and coastal waters that border Hawaii's shores. The waters around Hawaii are isolated from other reefs around the rest of the Pacific Ocean.

Picasso triggerfish

sandbar shark

scalloped hammerhead shark

yellowfin goatfish

sea urchins

whitetip reef shark

Almost 30 percent of
HAWAII'S FISH SPECIES
are found only here.

big longnose butterfly fish

manta ray

green sea turtle

Hawaiian monk seal

A DEEPER, DARKER ECOSYSTEM

Volcanoes continue to build new life on planet Earth even now, in the deepest depths of the ocean.

The tectonic plates of Earth's crust creep around the globe. Where two tectonic plates pull away from each other in opposite directions, they may create deep rift valleys.

In some of the deepest parts of the ocean, the sea floor spreads apart. There, plumes of magma rise up from inside the earth to fill the space. These are called rift volcanoes.

Deep-sea hydrothermal vents release mineral-rich plumes that look like smoke.

deep-sea shrimp

tube worm colony

In 1977, scientists exploring the deep ocean were amazed to discover a unique marine ecosystem within these undersea volcanic chains. Sunlight does not reach these depths. Bizarre forms of life have evolved here that do not depend on energy from the sun for photosynthesis. Instead, they use the energy from deep-sea volcanoes.

Within this ecosystem are hydrothermal vents—cracks in the ocean floor heated by magma from below. Unusual varieties of sea creatures reside here: deep-sea fish, octopuses, shrimp, crabs, worms, snails, and giant, red-tipped tube worms up to 6 feet (1.8 m) long. They all feast on a food chain that begins with the bacteria found in the boiling water that bubbles out of the volcanic vents.

FACT
Three-quarters of all volcanoes on Earth are located on the ocean floor.

PREDICTING THE FUTURE

Two and a half years after the 2018 eruption, Pele, the Goddess of Fire, stirred again. Kilauea sent lava, ash, and steam into the night sky in December 2020.

How can volcanologists know when Pele is going to display her destructive and creative powers again? They watch for telltale signs. These can be a series of small earthquakes known as earthquake swarms, a bulge growing on the side of the volcano, or magma rising in the caldera.

One of the goals of scientists who study volcanoes is to ensure that people who live near volcanoes stay safe. Like forest rangers keeping a lookout for fires and hurricane hunters flying into massive storms to collect data, volcanologists work to stay ahead of volcanic eruptions.

Kilauea's caldera at dusk

Volcanologists have some ways to help sense an upcoming eruption. Satellites measure changes in the shape and movement of the ground. These can help determine if magma may be on the move. Satellites can also detect hot spots or sulfur dioxide gas, which may hint that magma is rising toward the surface. Sensors on the volcanoes' slopes measure tiny earthquakes, slight tilts in the ground, and changes in the gases venting from cracks.

Warning signs like these have helped scientists make some successful forecasts in time to get residents to safety. But more work is needed to ensure a longer warning period before an eruption.

A scientist using a seismograph to measure volcanic activity at Hawaii Volcanoes National Park on the Big Island (left)

A satellite image taken of the Big Island from the International Space Station (below)

It still is not possible to predict the exact date that a volcano will erupt. But we are getting closer with sensors above and below ground to keep watch.

Each eruption gives volcanologists new clues about how volcanoes behave. Their findings help scientists improve their forecasts for the next time Pele decides to make her presence known.

Every single day,
the earth is alive with

ERUPTIONS

and

EARTHQUAKES.

On land and at the bottom of the ocean, volcanoes are bubbling, sputtering, or gushing lava, ash, and gases. These events remind us that we live on an ever-changing planet. As destructive as volcanic eruptions can be, these forces of nature create new land and new life—and new understanding of our Earth and our oceans.

Kilauea—and all the volcanoes that created the beautiful Hawaiian Islands—are proof enough that wonderful things can emerge from destruction.

GLOSSARY

Basalt is a dark-colored, fine-grained volcanic rock with low silica content that solidifies on the earth's surface. It makes up lava flows and the part of the earth's crust that forms the ocean floor. Rocks that have solidified from lava or magma are called igneous.

A **caldera** is a central depression or basin inside a volcano that forms when so much magma erupts that the volcano falls in on itself.

The **core** is the deepest layer of the earth, a very dense mass of hot metals such as iron and nickel. Earth's magnetic field is generated by circulation within the outer core, while the inner core is solid. The material in the layers of the earth become hotter and denser as depth increases.

The **crust** is the outermost layer of the earth; the solid, rocky surface of the earth.

Fissures are sideways cracks along the slope of a volcano from which lava flows, as opposed to lava erupting from a central crater.

A **food web** is a complex interrelationship of what eats what.

A **hot spot** is where plumes of magma from deep within the earth rise up and melt holes through the crust, like a blowtorch, to create volcanoes. Yellowstone, Iceland, and Hawaii are above hot spots.

A **hydrothermal vent** is a crack in the ocean floor heated by magma from below. Here, scientists discovered a food web that depends not on sunlight but on sulfur-producing bacteria that thrive inside the boiling water around volcanic vents.

Magma is a hot slushy mix of molten rock, crystals, and dissolved gases formed beneath the earth's surface. The more gases trapped in magma, the more likely it is that a volcanic eruption will be violent. Once magma erupts onto the surface it is called lava.

Magnitude is the size, extent, or importance of something, such as the intensity of an earthquake as measured by the Richter scale, which uses numbers from 1 to 9. Each number is equal to a tenfold increase in the magnitude of an earthquake, so a 6.0 earthquake is ten times stronger than a 5.0 quake.

The **mantle** is the middle layer of the earth. It is so hot that the rocks forming it can flow. Over millions of years, the mantle rises and falls in circular currents, much like soup heated on a stove.

Molten describes hot, liquefied rock.

Photosynthesis is the process where phytoplankton and other plants use a chemical called chlorophyll to capture the energy of sunlight and change it into food. In the process, they produce oxygen, which makes it possible for us to breathe.

Plankton are microscopic plants and floating animals that drift at the mercy of the waves, tides, and currents. Plankton feed, directly or indirectly, most other life in the sea.

A **plume** is an upwelling from deep within the mantle that can produce magma at the earth's surface.

Stromatolites are ancient sea creatures found inside the hot, steaming vents of underwater volcanoes. Over many millions of years, these simple, microscopic organisms were able to take carbon dioxide from the seawater and release oxygen. This helped to create an atmosphere where animals, eventually including humans, could breathe.

Sulfuric acid is a strong acid that can dissolve rocks and soil, destroy man-made structures, and poison air and water.

A **supervolcano** is an immense volcano capable of massive destruction when it erupts, sending ash, gases, and volcanic debris high into the atmosphere. Eruption of a supervolcano could have a worldwide impact.

Tectonic plates cause our planet to be constantly reshaped by volcanic eruptions, earthquakes, and mountain building. They are huge slabs of earth that slowly drift around the globe, like rafts propelled by currents of superheated magma. Their collisions can push up mountain ranges or create deep valleys and ocean trenches thousands of miles long.

A **tsunami** is a long-distance, fast-moving wave that may be triggered by an earthquake, volcanic eruption, or landslide. The sudden displacement of a large volume of water can generate powerful waves that can sweep across the entire ocean in a matter of hours.

SOURCE NOTES

p. 32, "The land is brand-new . . ." Misaki Takabayashi, "Coral Reefs Lost to Kīlauea Eruption," Dan Zukowski, *Sierra*, June 12, 2018, sierraclub.org/sierra/coral-reefs-lost-k-lauea-eruption
Accessed on March 23, 2021.

p. 32, "There's going to be renewal . . ." Steve Colbert, "How Volcanoes Reshape Ecosystems," Kim Steutermann Rogers, *Smithsonian Magazine*, August 9, 2018, smithsonianmag.com/science-nature/how-volcanoes-reshape-ecosystems-180969956/
Accessed on March 23, 2021.

SELECT BIBLIOGRAPHY

Personal Experiences

Discover Hawaii's Active Volcanoes field course, December 30, 2018–January 6, 2019, Hilo and environs, Hawaii, instructor Gary Lewis, geoetc.com, Personal communication

The Bernice Pauahi Bishop Museum, The Hawaii State Museum of Natural and Cultural History, Honolulu, Hawaii, bishopmuseum.org

Books

Cochran, Ford. *Wonders of the National Parks: A Geology of North America.* Chantilly, VA: The Great Courses, 2015.

Kane, Herb Kawainui. *Pele: Goddess of Hawaii's Volcanoes.* Captain Cook, HI: The Kawainui Press, 1987.

Lewis, Gary. *Discover the Wonders of Hawaiian Volcanoes.* Dallas, TX: Carte Diem Press, 2016.

TenBruggencate, Jan. *Hawaii: Land of Volcanoes.* Honolulu, HI: Mutual Publishing, 1999.

Articles and Websites

Bennett, Larisa, "Island Ecosystem Transformation via Lava," Smithsonian Ocean, 2018, ocean.si.edu/planet-ocean/seafloor/island-ecosystem-transformation-lava

Dvorsky, George, "Hawaii's Kilauea Volcano Unexpectedly Triggered a Gigantic Phytoplankton Bloom," Gizmodo.com, September 6, 2019, gizmodo.com/hawaii-s-kilauea-volcano-unexpectedly-triggered-a-gigan-1837929131

National Park Service, "Hawai'i Volcanoes," nps.gov/havo/learn/nature/volcanoes.htm

PBS, "Maine North America: Life," *Nova*, November 11, 2015, pbs.org/wgbh/nova/video/making-north-america-life/

PBS, "The Search for the Earliest Life," *Eons*, Season 1/ Episode 20, February 15, 2018, pbs.org/video/the-search-for-the-earliest-life-1wkbhq/

Science Education through Earth Observation for High Schools (SEOS), "Coral Reefs," seos-project.eu/coralreefs/coralreefs-c01-p05.html

Takabayashi, Misaki, Professional web page on University of Hawaii website, maunaloa.uhh.hawaii.edu/~misaki/About_Misaki_Takabayashi.html

Zukowski, Dan, "Coral Reefs Lost to Kīlauea Eruption," *Sierra*, June 12, 2018, sierraclub.org/sierra/coral-reefs-lost-k-lauea-eruption

All sites accessed on March 23, 2021.

INDEX

photo by Kevin Morris

Mary M. Cerullo describes herself as a science interpreter. She works with scientists and ocean advocates to explain scientific research and environmental issues to the public, with the goal of motivating others to protect the ocean. At times she has literally immersed herself in her work, diving among sharks in the Bahamas, studying dolphin behavior at the Dolphin Research Center in Florida, and most recently, exploring the connection between volcanoes and the ocean on the island of Hawaii.

Mary has written 21 award-winning books about the ocean for children, including the best-selling *Giant Squid: Searching for a Sea Monster*. She has worked with kids, teachers, and other ocean lovers for more than 40 years, from her first job at the New England Aquarium in Boston, to two decades with Friends of Casco Bay, an environmental advocacy organization in South Portland, Maine.